MARTY TWITTY

PRACTICAL GUIDE TO LEARN ALGORITHMS

Master Algorithmic Problem-Solving Techniques (2024 Guide for Beginners)

Copyright © 2024 by Marty Twitty

All rights reserved. No part of this publication may be reproduced, stored or transmitted in any form or by any means, electronic, mechanical, photocopying, recording, scanning, or otherwise without written permission from the publisher. It is illegal to copy this book, post it to a website, or distribute it by any other means without permission.

Marty Twitty asserts the moral right to be identified as the author of this work.

First edition

This book was professionally typeset on Reedsy. Find out more at reedsy.com

Contents

1	Introduction	1
2	Introduction to Algorithms	3
3	Types of Algorithms	14
4	Describing Algorithms	23
5	Error Handling	26
6	Analysis of Algorithms	34
7	An Introduction to Writing Programs	42
8	Types of Programming Languages	54
9	Important Programming Techniques	60
10	Testing the Program	73
11	Sorting and Searching Algorithms	78
12	Loop Control and Decision Making	100
13	Introduction to Data Structures	109
14	Comments and Formatting	118
15	Debugging	123
16	Conclusions	126

1

Introduction

To enter the realm of programming and coding successfully, it is essential to grasp the fundamental concepts. Without a solid understanding of programming, it is impossible to create intricate programs or products. At the core of every computer program lies an algorithm. To produce efficient and effective code, one must prioritize the formulation of algorithms, requiring a comprehensive comprehension of what an algorithm entails. This knowledge is crucial for the development of accurate programs. If there is uncertainty about the definition of an algorithm or a desire to revisit the basics, this resource is ideal. This comprehensive guide contains all the necessary information to comprehend algorithms and their application in crafting high-quality code and programs. The creation of the right algorithm is paramount, particularly for achieving perfection in code. An algorithm serves as a set of rules or instructions guiding a machine or computer through the necessary processes to attain a specific outcome.

Within the contents of this book, readers will gain insights into various algorithm types and their applicability in solving diverse problems. Additionally, the book introduces essential programming concepts that are integral to crafting precise code once an algorithm is established. Since algorithms serve as the foundation for any written code, it becomes imperative to incorporate specific statements to address various error types. The book provides guidance on this, offering insights into the lines of code necessary to handle errors effectively.

Common algorithms such as search, sort, loops, decision-making statements, and more are covered comprehensively in the book. Examples and programs are included to facilitate the conversion of algorithms into executable programs. It is emphasized that expertise in coding is unattainable without a solid grasp of the basics. Therefore, readers are encouraged to utilize the information in the book to enhance their coding understanding and practice regularly to master the art of crafting algorithms and programs.

The author expresses gratitude for the book purchase and hopes that it fulfills the reader's informational needs.

2

Introduction to Algorithms

Understanding what an algorithm is becomes crucial for a programmer as it guides how to employ it in coding. An algorithm constitutes a set of rules, instructions, or processes that any machine or system must adhere to when solving a problem. This may involve specifying operations, declaring variables, and, in simple terms, outlining steps to achieve desired outcomes.

Drawing a parallel, following a recipe equates to implementing an algorithm. Whether attempting a familiar or new dish, reading and precisely adhering to the provided instructions is essential for culinary success. Similar to cooking, where instructions ensure a dish's perfection, algorithms guarantee a system executes tasks accurately to produce the anticipated output. Algorithms, being straightforward instructions, can be implemented in any programming language, provided the syntax is understood, ensuring consistent outputs.

Association between Algorithms and Computer Science

The correlation between algorithms and computer science is evident. When you intend for a computer to execute a specific task, it necessitates the creation of a program. Through this program, you communicate precise instructions to the computer, specifying the actions it should perform to yield the desired output. Clarity in defining steps is crucial, as the computer diligently follows these instructions to achieve the intended result. It is essential to carefully select the appropriate input variables and information to provide the computer, ensuring the attainment of the correct output. In essence, algorithms stand out as the most effective method to accomplish a task.

Attributes of an Algorithm

Drawing a parallel to the realm of cooking, let's delve into the characteristics of an algorithm. Just as preparing a new dish involves following numerous instructions, algorithm creation shares a similar concept. While making your best effort to adhere to a recipe, you might improvise if a specific ingredient is unavailable. Similarly, it is crucial to note that not every statement in a program can be considered part of an algorithm.

Irrespective of the manner in which an algorithm is composed, it invariably possesses the following key characteristics:

1. **Feasibility**: Algorithms must embody simplicity, generality, and practicality. It is imperative to ensure that any programming language can execute the algorithm based on its available resources. Writing an algorithm without a comprehensive understanding of coding in a programming language is discouraged; it should be crafted based on pertinent information about its application.

2. **Finiteness**: Every algorithm should be finite. If loops or other functions are incorporated, it is essential to ensure that the algorithm concludes. Avoid the inclusion of infinite or circular references that might cause the algorithm to run incessantly.

3. **Language Independence**: No algorithm should exhibit dependence on a specific programming language. Instructions must be precise and straightforward, allowing the algorithm to be written in any programming language. As highlighted earlier, the output should remain consistent across different languages.

4. **Unambiguity**: Clarity and lack of ambiguity are paramount in every algorithm. Each step should possess unmistakable meaning, leaving no room for the compiler to consider multiple ways of executing a particular action. Every instruction should be crystal clear in all aspects.

5. **Well-Defined Inputs:** Just as preparing a dish requires meticulous attention to the relevant ingredients, defining inputs for an algorithm is equally crucial. Ensuring that inputs are precisely what is needed is fundamental to algorithmic

clarity.

6. **Well-Defined Outputs**: Similar to faithfully following a recipe to achieve the desired dish, an algorithm should clearly define the type of output it seeks to obtain. The output must be distinctly defined to avoid any ambiguity.

In summary, adhering to these characteristics ensures that an algorithm is not only effective but also versatile and comprehensible across various programming contexts.

Algorithm Design Process

Prior to embarking on the creation of any algorithm, it is essential to pose several crucial questions to guide the development process:

1. **Input Consideration**: Determine the inputs intended for utilization within the algorithm.
2. **Constraint Evaluation**: Identify any constraints relevant to the problem-solving endeavor.
3. **Expected Output Definition**: Clearly articulate the desired or anticipated output.
4. **Problem Identification**: Specify the problem being addressed through the algorithm.
5. **Solution within Constraints**: Outline the solution to the problem while adhering to identified constraints.

These inquiries serve as a framework to facilitate the generation of accurate outputs, promoting clear thinking for the creation of an effective algorithm. To illustrate this process, consider the example of crafting an algorithm for multiplying three numbers and displaying the resultant product.

Step One: Identifying the Problem Statement

Before delving into algorithmic design, addressing the aforementioned questions is paramount. Assume the objective is to formulate an algorithm for multiplying three numbers and computing the output – specifically, the product of these three numbers.

Once this initial step is accomplished, further elements must be defined, including the desired output, constraints, required inputs, and the solution in light of identified constraints. A key constraint involves ensuring user inputs solely consist of numbers for product calculation – necessitating three numeric inputs with the resulting output being their product. The proposed solution involves utilizing the multiplication operator '*' for the computation.

Step Two: Designing the Algorithm

Building upon the information gleaned from the preceding step, the algorithm design phase unfolds with the following steps:

1. Initiate the algorithm
2. Declare and initialize variables as y and z
3. Assign values to these variables, with the first, second, and third values assigned to x, y, and z, respectively
4. Declare and initialize an output variable to store the product of the input variables
5. Multiply the variables and store the product in the previously declared output variable
6. Print the output value
7. Conclude the algorithm

Step Three: Test the Algorithm

Subsequently, employing any programming language becomes instrumental for translating and executing the algorithm. Testing the algorithm's functionality within this context ensures its efficacy in delivering the desired outcome.

Selecting the Optimal Algorithm

When identifying the most suitable algorithm, consider the following criteria:

1. Accuracy: Ensure the algorithm consistently delivers the expected result, irrespective of how frequently it is utilized. An inaccurate algorithm may yield incorrect outputs or overlook certain input instances.

2. Constraint Recognition: Identify the various constraints relevant to the algorithm's development. Understanding and addressing these constraints are integral to creating a robust algorithm.

3. Efficiency Definition: Define the efficiency of the algorithm by considering the sequence in which inputs are utilized to achieve the desired output. The order of input usage significantly influences algorithmic efficiency.

4. Comprehensive Assessment: Evaluate and comprehend the computer architecture and the devices utilized to execute the algorithm. This understanding is crucial for optimizing the algorithm's performance on specific systems.

Grasping the Fundamental Algorithm Empowering Digital Life

Algorithms serve as directives for machines, guiding them through a sequence of instructions to attain solutions. They form the foundational framework for all technological advancements, offering solutions to diverse problems such as file compression, identifying relevant web pages during searches, or sorting lists. Beyond the immediate use of technology, contemporary education for children encompasses more than mere device operation. It involves exploring various algorithms that drive household televisions, smartphones, and even those underpinning social media platforms. Such exploration not only enhances programming skills but also fosters the creation of innovative technologies.

Algorithmic thinking emerges as a crucial skill, particularly when addressing complex mathematical and scientific challenges. This cognitive approach enables individuals to tackle problems systematically. For instance, when adding two numbers, algorithmic thinking involves considering the values of each number, determining where to store their sum, and devising the process for adding them. This exemplifies the basic application of algorithmic thinking.

Applying this thinking to more intricate problems, like long division, involves executing a series of algorithmic steps, including multiplication, subtraction, and division for each digit in the number being divided. Breaking down a problem into smaller components through algorithmic thinking simplifies the overall problem-solving process and allows for a targeted approach based on problem type.

Coding, regarded as an art form, plays a pivotal role in enhancing cognitive abilities. Engaging in diverse exercises and puzzles contributes to refining one's thought processes. Choosing activities that focus on conditional logic, sequencing, and repetition offers a comprehensive understanding of algorithmic principles, promoting effective problem-solving skills in various contexts.

INTRODUCTION TO ALGORITHMS

Crafting Your Personal Algorithm

For those with lengthy morning routines, consider simplifying tasks by designing a personalized algorithm. Establish small, achievable targets within the algorithm, disregarding any extraneous tasks. This approach introduces fundamental algorithmic concepts, including repetition (such as brushing the bottom row of teeth four times), sequencing (placing cereal in a bowl and then pouring milk), and conditional logic (refraining from eating if the bowl is empty).

To enhance algorithmic proficiency, add additional challenges, recognizing that computers lack an inherent understanding of intentions unless explicitly stated. Drawing a parallel with instructing a child, clarity in instructions is paramount – for instance, instructing them to add milk to cereal only after placing the milk-filled bowl in front of them. Failure to do so results in spilled milk, highlighting the importance of clarity in instructions for both humans and machines.

Consider experiences in arithmetic classes, where concepts like prime numbers and methods to ascertain a number's primality are learned. Applying this knowledge to a complex number, such as 123459734, necessitates multiple calculations. While utilizing a program can simplify this process, the effectiveness relies on the correctness of the underlying algorithm.

Advantages and Drawbacks

The majority of software developers employ algorithms as a foundational framework to conceptualize their approach to problem-solving before delving into code composition. While algorithms offer distinct advantages, they come with inherent drawbacks. This section will explore both the positive and negative aspects of utilizing algorithms.

Advantages:

1. Problem Segmentation: Algorithms enable the division of complex problems into more manageable segments. This facilitates the creation of algorithms and subsequent programming, tailored to the preferred programming language.

2. Precision: The procedural nature of algorithms ensures a precise and well-defined approach to problem-solving.

3. Step-by-Step Representation: An algorithm provides a systematic, step-by-step representation of problem-solving, making it easily comprehensible for a diverse audience.

4. Error Identification:Understanding an algorithm facilitates the identification of errors in the code, streamlining the debugging process.

5. Language Independence: Algorithms remain independent

of specific programming languages, enhancing accessibility for individuals with varying levels of programming knowledge.

Drawbacks:

1. Inadequacy for Large Programs: Algorithms prove impractical for explaining or representing extensive computer programs.

2. Additional Effort for Program Development: As algorithms are not inherently computer programs, extra effort is required to transform them into functional software.

3. Time-Consuming for Complex Algorithms: Crafting intricate algorithms demands a significant time investment, particularly for complex problem-solving scenarios.

3

Types of Algorithms

In this section, we will explore various categories of algorithms and their application in coding. The algorithmic types covered are as follows:

1. Backtracking algorithm
2. Brute Force algorithm
3. Divide and conquer algorithm
4. Dynamic programming algorithm
5. Greedy algorithm
6. Randomized algorithm
7. Simple recursive algorithm

Recursive Backtracking Approach

The utilization of a backtracking algorithm might present challenges, but comprehension of its fundamental concept facilitates easy program development. To illustrate, consider a problem divided into six smaller components. Initially addressing these smaller issues may not seemingly resolve the overarching problem. In such instances, a backtracking approach proves useful.

The strategy involves assessing subproblems to pinpoint the dependency of the main problem on a specific subproblem. By iteratively examining these subproblems, one can eventually arrive at a solution for the primary problem. The essence of this algorithm lies in revisiting the problem's outset if an immediate resolution proves elusive. Commencing with the first subproblem, if a solution remains elusive, backtracking to the beginning becomes imperative, initiating a fresh attempt at problem resolution.

A classic illustration of this algorithm is evident in the N Queens problem. Here, the goal is to strategically position queens on a chessboard, ensuring none can attack another. For clarity, let's explore a scenario with four queens, represented in a binary matrix denoting their positions:

{ 0, 0, 0, 1}
{ 0, 0, 1, 0}
{ 0, 1, 0, 0}
{ 1, 0, 0, 0}

The objective is to place queens in distinct columns, commencing with the leftmost column. Valid positions are determined by evaluating potential clashes with existing queens. If a suitable position is identified, the corresponding row and column are marked in a solution matrix. Failure to find an appropriate position necessitates a return to the starting point for a reattempt.

The algorithm unfolds as follows:

1. Place a queen in the leftmost column of the chessboard.
2. If queens can be placed without risk of mutual attacks, return true.
3. Systematically assess each row on the chessboard, executing the following: a. If a queen can be positioned in a row without clashes, record the row and column in a solution matrix. Check if a solution can be derived from this matrix. b. If a solution emerges, return true. c. If unsuccessful, remove the row and column from the solution matrix, exploring alternative combinations.
4. If all rows are exhausted without success, return false and revert to the initial step.

Exhaustive Search Approach

In employing the exhaustive search algorithm, one must meticulously examine every conceivable solution until identifying the optimal resolution for a given problem. This method involves scrutinizing all potential solutions to determine the best outcome. Upon discovering a viable solution, the algorithm can be promptly halted, and the identified resolution can be acknowledged. A prominent illustration of this approach is evident in the exact string-matching algorithm, where the objective is to locate a specific string within a given text.

Algorithmic Segmentation Technique

The divide and conquer algorithm, as implied by its name, involves breaking down a problem into multiple segments. Subsequently, a recursive function is applied to address these subproblems, and the obtained solutions are then integrated to derive the solution for the primary problem. Examples of the divide and conquer algorithm include the merge and quick sort algorithms, which will be explored in greater detail later in this book.

Utilizing the divide and conquer algorithmic approach provides the opportunity to address numerous subproblems simultaneously through parallelism. This is feasible because the subproblems are independent, allowing any algorithm developed with the divide and conquer technique to execute on various processes and machines concurrently. These algorithms rely on recursion, emphasizing the critical importance of memory management in their implementation.

Recursive Optimization Technique

The recursive optimization technique, commonly known as the dynamic programming algorithm, leverages historical information to formulate new solutions. Employing this algorithm facilitates the decomposition of intricate problems into more manageable subproblems, simplifying the overall problem-solving process. The algorithm's efficiency is enhanced by solving these smaller problems, and the outcomes are then utilized to address the overarching problem. Storing the results of subproblems in separate variables contributes to reducing the algorithm's runtime.

Illustrating this approach is a pseudocode example generating the Fibonacci series output:

Fibonacci(x)
If x = 0
Return 0
Else
Previous_Fibonacci = 0, Current_Fibonacci = 1
Repeat n-1 times
Next_Fibonacci = Previous_Fibonacci + Current_Fibonacci
Previous_Fibonacci = Current_Fibonacci
Current_Fibonacci = New_Fibonacci
Return Current_Fibonacci

In this example, the base value is set to zero. The problem is partitioned into distinct subproblems, and the results of these subproblems can be stored in other variables. To implement this, follow the steps below:

1. Define the solution and its structure.
2. Utilize recursion to articulate the solution.
3. Employ a bottom-up approach to compute the solution value.
4. Develop the optimal solution based on the computed results or information.

Efficient Solution Approach

Utilizing the greedy algorithm streamlines the process of breaking down a problem into smaller, manageable subproblems and determining optimal solutions for each. While this algorithm is effective, it's crucial to note that it may not always yield the absolute best solution for a given problem. Examples of the greedy algorithm include solving the Huffman coding problem and addressing money-counting scenarios.

Let's delve into the Huffman coding problem as an illustration. In this context, the goal is to compress data without sacrificing any information from the existing set. This involves assigning values to different input characters, with the resulting code length varying based on the frequency of usage. The algorithm involves two main steps: constructing the Huffman tree and traversing the tree to derive the solution.

Consider the input string "YYYZXXYYZ." By assessing character frequencies, it becomes apparent that "Y" has the highest occurrence, while "Z" is the least frequent. When coding in any programming language, "Y" will be assigned a shorter code than "Z," with the code's length influenced by the character's usage frequency.

Now, let's examine the input and output variables for a more extensive example:
   Input: A string with various characters - e.g., "BCCBEBFFFF ADCEFLLKLKKEEBFF"
   Output: Assigning codes to each character:

- Data: F, Frequency: 7, Code: 01
- Data: L, Frequency: 3, Code: 0001
- Data: K, Frequency: 3, Code: 0000
- Data: C, Frequency: 3, Code: 101
- Data: B, Frequency: 4, Code: 100
- Data: D, Frequency: 1, Code: 110
- Data: E, Frequency: 4, Code: 001

Algorithm for constructing the tree:

1. Declare and initialize a string with diverse characters.
2. Assign codes to each character in the string.
3. Build the Huffman tree.

a. Define each node based on character, frequency, and left/right child.
   b. Create a frequency list with initial frequencies set to zero.
   c. Iterate through the string, updating frequencies in the list.
   d. If frequency is non-zero, add the character to the tree node with a priority label.
4. If the priority list is not empty, assign the item to the left node; otherwise, assign it to the right node.
5. Traverse the node to find the assigned code.
6. End the algorithm.

For tree traversal, use the following input:

1. Huffman tree and node.
2. Code assigned to the node.

The output provides the character and its corresponding code based on the traversal conditions.

Stochastic Algorithm Overview

When employing a randomized algorithm, decisions are made using random numbers to address specific algorithms. An illustration of this approach is evident in the quicksort algorithm, which we'll explore further in subsequent sections of this book.

Fundamental Recursive Algorithm Approach

Utilizing a basic recursive algorithm provides a straightforward means to address various problems efficiently. This algorithm is commonly applied in conjunction with other algorithms. Each iteration of a simple recursive algorithm involves a reduction in input value. Establishing a base value is crucial, signaling the system to terminate the algorithm. This method proves effective for problem-solving as long as the problem is divisible into homogeneous segments. An example involves computing the factorial of a number, as depicted in the following pseudocode:

    Factorial(number)
    If number is 0
    Return 1
    Else
    Return (number * Factorial(number – 1))
    The base value, set at zero, signifies algorithm termination

when the output value reaches zero. Examining the concluding part of the algorithm reveals the systematic breakdown of the problem into smaller, manageable segments for resolution.

4

Describing Algorithms

Effectively articulating algorithms is crucial as it is the sole means of problem resolution. In the preceding chapter, we delved into various algorithms and their application in problem-solving. Most of the discussed algorithm types in the previous chapter involved breaking down problems into more manageable segments, facilitating the resolution of the core issue. It is imperative to select an algorithm that aligns with your needs, ideally requiring minimal or no alterations to the program's data structures.

For instance, when employing the bubble sort algorithm, it is essential to store the pertinent information in an array or another suitable data structure. Utilizing comparison and exchange operations, you can then update the data accordingly. A more in-depth examination of the bubble sort algorithm will follow later in this book.

If data structures are part of your strategy, a clear description of the structure streamlines the construction process. Consider the merge sort algorithm, which allows faster information comparison in the dataset than the quick sort algorithm. However, employing a linked list data structure is necessary for efficient sorting, significantly enhancing algorithm performance.

Incorporate all requisite details when employing a merge sort algorithm, covering error checking, error handling, and pointer manipulation. While achieving a balance between abstraction and specificity is challenging when describing an algorithm, comprehensive detailing becomes imperative during code composition. Leaving the algorithm as a black box is discouraged. Even if you possess proficient coding skills or collaborate with a skilled programmer, providing a detailed explanation enhances clarity.

When enhancing algorithm details, consider the following aspects:

1. Algorithm Purpose:
 - Define the functions the algorithm is designed to perform on the code or data.

2. Data Structures:
 - Specify any required data structures for manipulating information within the algorithm.

3. Step Descriptions:
 - Clearly outline steps and incorporate details, ensuring comprehensibility for any reader.

4. Correctness Justification:
 - Offer a rationale for the correctness of the algorithm to

instill confidence.

5. Performance Analysis:
   - Evaluate the algorithm's speed, cost, space utilization, and other relevant metrics.

Adapting the algorithm description based on the audience and purpose is paramount. When introducing a new algorithm for a well-known problem, emphasize the technique, correctness justification, and comparative analysis. Showcase the superiority of your algorithm over the incumbent one. Similarly, when introducing a novel data structure, elucidate the reasons for its adoption and outline the planned analysis methodology.

Leveraging tools to validate algorithm correctness contributes significantly to a more articulate description. Neglecting this aspect should be avoided for a comprehensive and effective portrayal of the algorithm.

5

Error Handling

As previously highlighted, addressing errors in any algorithm or code is crucial. The concept is straightforward—identify specific lines of code to manage errors and exceptions. Utilizing keywords like 'null' can simplify error and exception handling, although it's essential to note that programming languages may interpret such keywords differently. While it's vital to incorporate proper error-handling code, if doing so complicates the logic, it's advisable to keep the error handling separate from the main code. Consider the following tips:

- Incorporate the 'catch' keyword at the appropriate location in the code to pinpoint errors. Use the 'try' keyword to mark the code section where errors might occur. Establish a try-catch-finally statement to encapsulate the error-handling code.
   - When introducing an exception in the code, provide sufficient information for the compiler to identify the error's position. Craft an informative error message and pass it to the exception. Verify that the code's operation aligns with the expected outcome.

- Rather than directing the compiler to a block of error code within the program, opt for throwing an exception. By doing so, you prompt the compiler to scrutinize the code for issues and debug it. If you choose to include error-handling code, ensure clear awareness of its placement. Throwing exceptions when errors arise enhances code debugging efficiency and minimizes potential issues.

Examining for Anomalies

Regrettably, programming languages seldom provide an exhaustive catalog of distinct exception and error handling methodologies. Nonetheless, it is imperative to make a concerted effort to comprehend and employ these techniques effectively in code error management. When crafting an algorithm, incorporate these error-handling methods. A scrutinized exception facilitates ensuring that the signature of each function or method within the code delineates every exception intended for transference to the caller.

It is pivotal to note that the compiler will abstain from executing the code if the signature fails to align. The subsequent illustration illustrates how to employ exception and error handling codes in Java:

```
public void ioOperation(boolean isResourceAvailable) throws IOException
{
if (!isResourceAvailable) {
throw new IOException();
```

```
}
}
```

A drawback associated with this type of exception lies in its potential infringement of certain programming language rules. If any checked exception can be thrown using a method in the code, and the catch is positioned three lines above the code, declaring an exception in the method's signature becomes necessary. Consequently, certain code blocks may undergo modification due to the incorporation of exception handling or error handling segments.

Establishing Exception Definitions

The paramount task lies in crafting precise exceptions within the code aligned with the functional requisites. The question arises: How will errors be categorized? Is the classification contingent upon their nature, distinguishing between network failure, programming error, or device malfunction? Alternatively, is the classification rooted in their origin, shedding light on the source of these errors? Perhaps, error classification is based on how the compiler identifies and categorizes these errors?

Certain programming languages facilitate the transformation of existing code blocks into exception or error handling code. The subsequent example illustrates this process:

```
class LocalPort {
private let innerPort: ACMEPort
func open() throws {
```

```
do {
try innerPort.open()
} catch let error as DeviceResponseError {
throw PortDeviceFailure.portDeviceFailure(error: error)
} catch let error as ATM1212UnlockedError {
throw PortDeviceFailure.portDeviceFailure(error: error)
} catch let error as GMXError {
throw PortDeviceFailure.portDeviceFailure(error: error)
}
}
}
```

Special Scenarios in Patterns

In the realm of programming languages, there exists the capability to construct or configure an object, assigning it the responsibility of managing specific categories of errors within the code. This ensures that the client or primary code remains shielded from any exceptional behavior.

Having delved into diverse methods of handling code, let's shift our focus to the utilization of the null keyword for error management.

Null Values

Injecting the null keyword into a method renders the code challenging to debug and should be avoided. Incorporating null values into error-handling code introduces additional complexities. When the output manifests as a null value, the task of pinpointing its origin within your code becomes burdensome.

```swift
// Un-swifty, but matches code in the book
    func register(item: Item?) {
    if item != nil {
    let registry: ItemRegistry? = persistentStore.getItemRegistry()
    if registry != nil {
    let existingItem = registry.getItem(item.getId())
    if existingItem.getBillingPeriod().hasRetailOwner() {
    existingItem.register(item)
    }
    }
    }
    }
```

```swift
// More Swifty using guard statements.
    func register(item: Item?) {
    guard let item = item,
    let registry = persistentStore.getItemRegistry() else {
    return
    }
    let existingItem = registry.getItem(item.getId())
    guard existingItem.getBillingPeriod().hasRetailOwner() else {
    return
    }
    existingItem.register(item)
```

Common Error Messages

Creating uncomplicated programs makes compilation a straightforward task. If you adhere to the algorithm and correctly employ variables in your code, it may seem like errors are unlikely to occur. However, overconfidence is unwarranted, as programmers typically dedicate a significant portion of their time rectifying flaws within their programs—a process commonly known as debugging. This section delves into diverse error-handling techniques applicable to any written program.

Editing and Recompiling

Spelling issues in your code can trigger compiler errors. While seemingly trivial, these errors demand your attention, and rectifying them is crucial. Embrace the learning process that accompanies resolving errors, following these steps to rerun your code:

- Reedit the source code and save the file to disk.
- Recompile the code.
- Run the program.

Encountering multiple errors during code re-editing is normal; however, understanding and addressing these errors will lead you to step 3—running the program successfully.

Reedit the Source Code

Modifying the source code file is a frequent necessity to overcome error messages encountered during compilation.

Changes might involve altering on-screen messages or introducing new features.

Recompile

Running the program after code modifications requires compiling it anew. Link the program to the compiler and, since the code has changed, link it first before sending it to the compiler. If the compiler throws an error, repeat the process. Use the following command prompt code for recompilation:

gcc hello.c -o hello

Upon successful compilation without error messages, consider your code error-free.

Dealing with Errors

Accepting that errors are inevitable in coding is crucial. Instead of fretting over errors, embrace them as valuable learning experiences to prevent recurring mistakes. The compiler aids in pinpointing the exact line where errors occur, facilitating easy resolution.

Consider the example below:

#include

int main() {
   printf("This program will err.\n")
   return 0;
}

Compile this code and observe the error message. While the message may initially seem cryptic, it provides essential information:

- The error occurred before the "return" keyword.

- The error is in line 5 of the code.
- The code with the error is saved as "error.c."
- The type of error is identified.

Understanding these details helps identify and fix errors efficiently. In this example, a missing semicolon at the end of the fifth line causes a parse or syntax error. Edit the source code, save the changes, and continue refining your ability to identify and address errors in your code. With practice, you'll become adept at swiftly debugging your programs.

6

Analysis of Algorithms

Evaluating the intricacy of an algorithm holds significance. When delving into algorithm analysis, focus on the asymptotic aspect for evaluation. This entails examining how the algorithm's functions operate when dealing with extensive datasets. The term "analysis of algorithms" was coined by Donald Knuth.

The foundation of computational complexity theory lies in algorithm analysis, providing a theoretical estimation of the resources an algorithm requires. As established in prior chapters, the input for any algorithm must have arbitrary length. Analyzing an algorithm involves assessing the time and memory space needed for its execution.

The efficiency or running time of an algorithm is denoted as a variable in the time complexity function, while the memory usage is expressed as a variable in the space complexity function.

Significance of Algorithm Analysis

The rationale behind analyzing an algorithm becomes apparent when confronted with a problem susceptible to multiple solutions. Choosing an algorithm to address a specific problem allows the development of a pattern applicable to analogous problems.

Distinguishing between algorithms is crucial, even when their objectives align. Each algorithm varies in terms of time and memory utilization. For instance, when sorting a list of numbers, the selection of a sorting algorithm from various options will yield different comparison times, implying disparate time complexities. Memory space occupied by an algorithm is also a critical consideration.

Conducting an analysis of an algorithm is imperative to gauge its problem-solving efficacy. Evaluation should encompass memory size utilization, with the primary focus on performance and runtime. Several tests and analyses aid in this assessment:

1. Worst-case: Evaluating the algorithm's performance under conditions necessitating the maximum number of steps for a given input.
2. Amortized: Applying a sequence of operations to the input over a specific timeframe.

3. Average case: Determining the average steps needed, considering both minimum and maximum, for a given input.
4. Best-case: Assessing the scenario where the algorithm achieves the expected output with the minimum number of steps for a given input.

Balancing space and time complexity is essential for problem-solving. Operating within a system with constrained memory, one must account for both program execution and data storage. Notably, different algorithms exhibit trade-offs between space and time. A comparison of the bubble sort and merge sort algorithms reveals that the former demands more space for variable storage. Consequently, the bubble sort algorithm takes longer than the merge sort algorithm, suggesting the suitability of each depending on the specific resource constraints – choosing merge sort for time efficiency and bubble sort for memory conservation.

Methods of Algorithmic Analysis

To evaluate how an algorithm utilizes resources, consider the following strategies:

Asymptotic Analysis:
This analysis examines how an algorithm behaves with changing input sizes. It disregards small input values, focusing solely on larger values. An algorithm is deemed superior when it exhibits a very slow asymptotic growth rate. However, this

is not universally applicable. For example, comparing a linear algorithm and a quadratic algorithm reveals the linear one as asymptotically better, given its more efficient use of variables to achieve the objective.

Recurrence Equations:

Various recurrence equations describe an algorithm's functioning with smaller input values, especially relevant for divide and conquer algorithms. Consider a function T(n) denoting the running time for any problem with an input size of N. If n is consistently small across subproblems, the solution takes constant time denoted as θ(1). For numerous subproblems with input size n/b, the algorithm takes time T(n/b) * a. The time calculation follows the equation:

$$T(n) = \left\{ \begin{array}{ll} \theta(1) & \text{if } n \leq c \\ aT(n/b) + D(n) + C(n) & \text{otherwise} \end{array} \right.$$

Methods to solve a recurrence relation include the Recursion Tree Method, Substitution Method, and Master's Theorem.

Amortized Analysis:

This analysis is applied to algorithms with similar operation sequences, offering a range or bound of the overall algorithm's running cost. It does not specify individual operation bounds, focusing on the algorithm's efficiency and design.

Aggregate Method:

Taking a holistic approach, this method considers the overall problem. If an algorithm executes n operations, each taking time T(n), the amortized cost for each operation, denoted as T(n)/n, represents the worst-case scenario.

Accounting Method:
Assign a cost to each operation based on its actual cost. If the actual cost is less than the amortized cost, the difference serves as credit, available to cover operations with costs exceeding the amortized cost. The formula is $\sum_{i=1}^{n} c_i \geq \sum_{i=1}^{n} c_i$.

Potential Method:
Similar to the accounting method, this method considers the algorithm's work as potential energy, viewing the total cost in terms of energy. The amortized cost is calculated using the formula $\sum_{i=1}^{n} c_i^1 = \sum_{i=1}^{n} (c_i + \Phi(D_i) - \Phi(D_{i-1})) = \sum_{i=1}^{n} c_i + \Phi(D_n) - \Phi(D_0)$.

Dynamic Table:
When an algorithm lacks sufficient memory for input and output variables, data may be moved to a large table. Amortized analysis helps calculate the cost of constant insertion and deletion, determining if it exceeds a specified threshold.

Space Complexity

As previously mentioned, each algorithm consumes memory space, particularly during execution. This section delves into strategies for managing intricate calculations that aid in evaluating an algorithm's space requirements. Similar to time complexity, space complexity enables the classification of algorithms based on computational intricacies.

When analyzing an algorithm, it is crucial to examine its space complexity function. This function delineates the space utilized by the algorithm during its execution, encompassing memory occupied by input, temporary, or output variables. In algorithm design, consideration should be given to the additional memory required for storing both input and output, an aspect often overlooked by programmers.

To gauge input variables' memory, employ fixed-length variables, using a specific number of integers or bytes. Any function devised for this purpose remains independent of actual memory space. While time complexity often takes precedence, neglecting space complexity can impede program functionality due to insufficient memory space.

Understanding Recursion

While we covered a basic recursive algorithm earlier in this book, let's delve deeper into the concept of recursion. This section aims to demystify recursive algorithms and equip you with insights to easily recognize them.

A recursive function can be likened to a black box, revealing only its intended outcomes. When dealing with such a function, you comprehend its purpose but lack a detailed understanding of its internal processes. For instance, if tasked with utilizing a function to sort elements in an array, your directive might be articulated as follows: 'Apply the merge sort algorithm to arrange elements in an array in ascending order, using another array.'

Breaking down such algorithms into smaller problems facilitates comprehension before tackling the overarching issue. For example, envision the machine independently sorting elements in one array before transferring them to another. Alternatively, you can segment the array, sort its elements individually, and subsequently merge them into a unified array.

This description is adaptable and applicable to various sorting algorithms, be it merge sort or quick sort. The distinguishing factor among these algorithms lies in their data division and sorting methods. Quick sort employs intricate partitioning coupled with straightforward merging, while merge sort follows the opposite approach.

It's imperative to define boundary conditions when implementing a recursive algorithm to halt the recursion. Building on the earlier example, as you segment the array, smaller arrays may emerge, containing just one or two elements—such arrays don't necessitate sorting. When employing the insertion sort algorithm, a divide and conquer strategy is employed to segment the sequence, sort individual segments, and ultimately merge the entire list.

Providing a comprehensive explanation of the algorithm during discussions about its overview is paramount. This elucidation serves as the key to determining the functions and methods to employ. Regardless of the chosen algorithmic strategy, articulating a description and rationale for opting for a particular method over others is essential.

7

An Introduction to Writing Programs

For individuals new to programming, there are crucial considerations before translating an algorithm into a program. This chapter elucidates these concepts, guiding you on utilizing various operators and data types to execute functions effectively.

Programming Principles:

Programmers typically write code for specific projects, aiming for clarity and comprehension. Adhering to specific principles ensures the production of high-quality code. Some key principles include:

1. Naming Conventions: Accurate naming of functions, methods, and variables is paramount for error-free code. Descriptive names facilitate understanding, enhancing code readability. Prefix Boolean variables with 'is' for clarity.

For instance, in a banking application handling payments:

double totalBalance; // Represents the user account balance
double amountToDebit; // Represents the amount to charge the user
double amountToCredit; // Represents the amount to give to the user
boolean isUserActive;

Follow camel case for data structures and variables, and use screaming snake case for constants.

1. File Structure: Maintaining project structure aids comprehension. Though structures differ, consistency is key for seamless understanding.
2. Functions and Methods: Choosing the right methods and functions is pivotal. Follow these rules for naming functions:

- Use camel case.
- Place the method name on the same line as the opening bracket.
- Name functions using a non-verb sound.
- Ensure functions use one or two arguments at most.

```
double getUserBalance(long int accountNumber) {
    // Method Definition
}
```

1. **Indentation**: Indentation enhances code readability, especially for nested structures or code written outside a method.
2. **Avoid Self-Explanation**: Write comments to explain

code functionality. Avoid self-explanatory comments that don't add value.

```
javaCopy code
final double PI = 3.14; // This is pi value //
```

1. **KISS** (Keep It Simple Silly): Simplicity is key. Develop systems that are as straightforward as possible, avoiding unnecessary complexities.
2. **DRY** (Don't Repeat Yourself): Write unambiguous code. Avoid redundancy to make code decipherable without excessive effort.
3. **YAGNI** (You Aren't Gonna Need It): Add functions and operations only if necessary. Stick to what is essential for effective code, aligning with unit testing, integration, and refactoring.
4. **Logging**: Break and test code sections, creating logs for debugging. Log statements within functions assist in understanding their success or failure.

Following these principles ensures the creation of well-structured, readable, and efficient code.

Objects and Categories

Categories

A category serves as a design plan, giving rise to an object. Various types of variables exist within a category:

- **Class**: Declared in a class and outside any method using the static keyword.
  - **Class variables**: Declared in classes, not within any method, utilizing the static keyword.
  - **Local variables**: Defined within a block, method, or constructor, termed local variables. Declaration occurs in the class, and initialization takes place in the method. Once the method completes, the variable is removed from computer memory.
  - **Instance:** A variable defined within a class but outside a method. These are initialized during class instantiation and are accessible from within methods, blocks, or constructors of the class.

Categories can encompass multiple methods for accessing various values. In the context of a person, "eating()" is an example of a method.

Entities

Entities surround us, such as dogs, humans, buildings, and houses. Each object possesses its unique characteristics, behavior, and state. For instance, considering a dog, attributes like name, color, and breed are part of its state, while behaviors include running, barking, and tail wagging. A software object mirrors this pattern, having its own state stored in a field and behavior indicated by methods.

Creating Entities

As previously mentioned, an entity originates from a category, and the new keyword is used to define it in the class. The following steps outline entity creation:

- **Declaration:** Declare a variable with a name and define the object type in the code.
    - **Instantiation:** Utilize the new keyword to create an object.
    - **Initialization**: A constructor call follows the new keyword, initializing the object.

To access an instance method or variable, an object must be created. The pathway for accessing the instance variable involves creating the object, referencing the constructor, and then accessing the variable or method.

Constructors

Constructors play a vital role in a category, with each class having one. If a constructor isn't explicitly written, Java provides a default constructor. When creating a new entity, the compiler automatically invokes the constructor. The key rule for a constructor is its name matching the class, and a class may have more than one constructor. Programming languages allow the use of singleton classes, restricting instantiation to only one instance.

Source File Declaration

Understanding source file rules, especially when declaring a class in the code, is crucial. Key considerations include:

- A source file can have numerous non-public classes.
  - In a class defined within a package, the first statement in the source file must be the package statement.
  - Only one public class is permitted in any source file.
  - Import statements, if included, should appear between the class declaration and the package statement. Without a package statement, the import statement is the first line.
  - The source file and public class must share the same name, with the file name extended by the programming language's extension.
  - Package and import statements apply to all classes in the source file, with no variation allowed.

Categorization and import statements serve to streamline the programming process, making it more manageable. The import statement guides the compiler to locate a specific class accurately.

Types of Data

Data represents a collection of instructions, ideas, and facts presented in a specific format, capable of interpretation, communication, or processing by a machine. Special characters and groups of characters serve as the means to express this data.

When data is classified or organized, it transforms into information, which is essentially processed data. Every decision or action is based on this information, imbuing it with meaning for the recipient. To ensure meaningful decision-making, processed data must meet certain criteria:

- Completeness: Information should encompass all relevant parameters and data.
    - Accuracy: Information should consistently be correct.
    - Timeliness: Information should be readily available whenever needed.

Data Processing Cycle

Data processing involves the reordering or restructuring of data by a machine, enhancing its utility and value. The data processing cycle comprises three steps:

1. **Input:**
    - Data is fed into the machine.
    - Preparation of input data is necessary to convert it into a

machine-readable form.

- Electronic computers may record input data on various media like magnetic disks, pen drives, tapes, etc.

2. **Processing:**

- Data from the previous step is restructured to generate more useful information.

- Examples include calculating a paycheck based on time cards or summarizing sales based on sales orders.

3. **Output:**

- The final step collects data from the previous step.

- The format of the data is determined based on its intended use.

Variables

A variable is a reserved memory location used for storing values. When creating a new variable, memory space is automatically reserved, with the amount determined by the variable type. Variables can store decimals, integers, or characters, with two main data types in every programming language:

1. **Primitive:**

- Most high-level programming languages include eight primitive data types.

- These predefined types, named with keywords, cover integers, long values, floats, doubles, bytes, shorts, booleans, and characters.

2. **Reference or Object:**
- Reference variables, created using constructors, access objects and are declared as specific immutable types.
- Reference objects encompass class objects and various array variables, with a default null value.

Literals

Literals serve as a source code representation of fixed values, expressed directly in the code without computation. Primitive data types can be assigned literals, and different number systems (octal, decimal, hexadecimal) can be used. String literals, represented as sequences of characters enclosed in double quotes, also support escape sequences.

Data Manipulation Operations

In coding, diverse operators play a pivotal role in manipulating data and variables. This section delves into the various operators along with their functionalities.

Logical Operators

These operators deal with logical conditions:

- && (logical and): Evaluates true if both operands are non-zero values.
   - || (logical or): Evaluates true if either operand is non-zero.
   - ! (logical not): Evaluates false if a condition is true, reversing the logical state of the operand.

Arithmetic Operators

Utilized for mathematical expressions, these operators align with familiar symbols:

-+: Addition.
   - -: Subtraction (right operand subtracted from the left).
   - ***: Multiplication.
   - /: Division (left operand divided by the right).
   - %: Modulus (remainder of the division of the left operand by the right).
   - ++: Increment (increases operand value by 1).
   - —: Decrement (decreases operand value by 1).

Assignment Operators

These operators facilitate the assignment of values:

- =: Assigns the value from the right operand to the left.
   - +=: Adds the value of the right operand to the left and assigns the result to the left.

- -=: Subtracts the right from the left operand and assigns the result to the left.
- \=: Multiplies the right with the left operand and assigns the result to the left.
- /=: Divides the left operand by the right and assigns the result to the left.
- %=: Takes the modulus of two operands and assigns the result to the left.
- «=: Left shift and assignment.
- »=: Right shift and assignment.

Relational Operators

These operators ascertain relationships between operands:

- == (equal to): Checks if the values of operands are equal; evaluates true if they are.
- != (not equal to): Checks if the values of operands are not equal; evaluates true if they differ.
- > (greater than): Checks if the left operand is greater than the right; evaluates true if it is.
- < (less than): Checks if the left operand is less than the right; evaluates true if it is.
- >= (greater than or equal to): Checks if the left operand is greater than or equal to the right; evaluates true if it is.
- <= (less than or equal to): Checks if the left operand is less than or equal to the right; evaluates true if it is.

Operator Precedence

Operator precedence dictates the order of evaluation in expressions. Higher precedence is given to certain operators over others, such as multiplication over addition. The order of precedence, from highest to lowest, is crucial in understanding how expressions are processed:

- **Postfix:**>() [] . (dot operator) – Left to right
  - **Unary**: >++ - - ! ~ – Right to left
  - **Multiplicative:**>* / – Left to right
  - **Additive:** >+ - – Left to right
  - **Shift:**»> »> « – Left to right
  - **Relational:**» >= < <= – Left to right
  - **Equality:**>== != – Left to right
  -**Logical AND**: >&& – Left to right
  - **Logical OR**: >|| – Left to right
  - **Conditional**: >?: – Right to left
  - **Assignment:** >= += -= *= /= %= »= «= &= ^= |= – Right to left

8

Types of Programming Languages

Diverse Programming Languages and Their Characteristics

A multitude of programming languages has emerged, with ongoing development to cater to various purposes, such as R and Python, designed specifically for data analytics. With this proliferation, understanding the strengths and weaknesses, along with the distinctive traits of each language, becomes crucial. Programming languages can be categorized based on preferred programming styles, and while numerous languages are introduced annually, only a select few gain popularity, becoming staples in the toolkit of professional programmers.

Programming languages play a pivotal role in governing machine and computer performance. Each language is unique, and this chapter explores the different types of programming languages. By assimilating the information presented here, individuals can discern the type of programming language that aligns with their requirements.

Defining Programming Languages

To embark on an exploration of various programming languages, it's essential to grasp the definition of a programming language. A programming language serves as a means to instruct machines or computers to execute specific functions. Some programmers refer to these languages as notations, as they are employed to articulate algorithms and regulate machine performance. The versatility of programming languages allows the expression of algorithms in different ways. With nearly a thousand programming languages in existence, they may take on an imperative or declarative form based on usage, further categorized into syntax and semantics.

Categories of Programming Languages

Within this section, we will explore distinct classifications of programming languages. Each programming language neatly fits into one of these identified categories.

Procedural Programming Language

Commonly employed by programmers who design algorithms, procedural programming languages involve specifying the sequence of instructions or statements guiding the machine.

Distinguished by robust loops, multiple variables, and other components, this language contrasts with functional programming languages. In procedural languages, control over variables is often based on values returned by methods or functions. Syntaxes and statements within this language can be utilized for tasks such as information printing.

Functional Programming Language

Relying on stored data within the computer, a functional programming language opts for recursive functions instead of loops. The primary goal of this language is to leverage the return values of methods or functions, emphasizing a distinct approach from procedural languages.

Logic Programming Language

Designed for declarative statements, a logic programming language enables programmers to articulate instructions comprehensible to the machine. By utilizing efficient algorithms, this language streamlines the execution of functions, requiring less computational space. In using this programming language, explicit instructions on how the computer should execute a function are unnecessary, as the language imposes restrictions on the machine's thought process.

Programming Languages

Pascal Language

Pascal serves as a programming language commonly introduced in educational settings, though its usage in industries has dwindled. Distinguishing itself from most languages, Pascal opts for key phrases and words instead of braces and symbols, rendering it more accessible for beginners compared to languages like C and C++. Additionally, Pascal supports object-oriented programming through Delphi, and it remains the exclusive choice for Borland, a software company.

Fortran Language

Widely embraced by scientists, Fortran facilitates numerical computations with ease. It allows straightforward variable storage regardless of memory size and is preferred by data scientists and engineers for accurate calculations and predictions. While writing programs in Fortran can be challenging, mastering the language is essential for effective coding due to its sometimes intricate core logic.

Java Language

Functioning as a versatile, cross-platform language, Java excels in various networking tasks and finds application in Java-based web platforms. Its syntax similarity to C++ enables developers to create applications across different platforms seamlessly. Java's object-oriented nature allows for diverse product and application development. While earlier versions limit heavy code writing, recent updates provide features that simplify the creation of efficient and concise programs.

Perl Language

Primarily associated with the Unix operating system, Perl is frequently utilized for file and directory management. Its popularity stems from its Common Gateway Interface (CGI) programming feature, employed by web servers to enhance website capabilities. Perl's simplicity and CGI compatibility make it a preferred choice for web hosting services over C++, as a single Perl script file can host multiple websites.

PHP Language

As a scripting language, PHP specializes in designing web applications and pages. Its features include linking websites to different databases, website reconstruction, and generating HTTP headers. With its set of components, PHP facilitates object-oriented functionality, simplifying the development of websites.

LISP Language

Favored by many programmers, LISP accommodates various data structures, such as lists and arrays, with an easy-to-understand syntax. This flexibility enables the creation of new data structures and the execution of functions not feasible in other programming languages.

Scheme Language

Serving as an alternative to LISP, Scheme boasts straightforward features with an easily graspable syntax. While it can be re-implemented in other languages, especially LISP, Scheme is primarily utilized for solving uncomplicated problems where syntax complexity is not a concern.

C++ Language

Recognized as an object-oriented programming language, C++ finds prominence in building large applications. Programmers can divide complex programs into smaller sections for more manageable development. The efficiency of using one block of code multiple times is a hallmark of this language, although opinions on its efficiency may vary among developers.

C Language

A widely adopted programming language, C is known for its simplicity, making it accessible to almost anyone. Programmers often prefer C for its faster program execution. Leveraging different features, C enables the development of efficient programs with the right algorithms. Its popularity persists, in part, because it allows users to incorporate features from C++. In this exploration of various programming languages, including Pascal, Fortran, C, C++, Scheme, and others, we have examined their applications and differences. It is crucial to select the most suitable language for the specific program or product under development.

9

Important Programming Techniques

Given the proliferation of various programming languages, determining the optimal language for use becomes a challenging task. Each programming language serves distinct purposes, yet the crux lies in prioritizing the syntax, as it holds greater significance. Equally crucial is understanding how a programming language is structured and comprehending the meanings and applications of different terms.

Arrays

Arrays, as collections of variables sharing the same data type, play a vital role. Each element within an array is allocated an index, enabling efficient retrieval of specific elements using these indices. For instance, generating random numbers allows the retrieval of a corresponding item, like a day of the week, by utilizing the associated index.

Certain programming languages lack support for data structures like arrays, but this functionality can be replicated using lists or tuples. Sparse arrays can employ binary trees, although this method may seem intricate. In languages such as JavaScript, array indices can serve as Boolean operators, facilitating the use of various binary expressions for condition evaluation, simplifying the selection of values without resorting to conditional statements.

An array, also known as a multivariable, permits the storage of variables of the same data type together. Declaring arrays follows the same syntax as other variables in a program. For instance, the declaration "float array1[10]" indicates an array capable of holding ten values. Values can be assigned to the array using the syntax "float array1[] = {53.0, 88.0, 96.7, 93.1, 89.5}," where this array comprises five float data type values.

Each element in the array functions as an independent variable within functions or modules, termed as elements. These elements are assigned specific positions known as indices, with the index of the first element being zero. Values are assigned to the array in a manner similar to regular variables. Notably, every program has a fixed array size, and determining the dimension involves assigning a specific length to the array.

Constructing Extensive Programs

When crafting programs, the option exists to create both small and large-scale applications. Although there's nothing inherently wrong with developing sizable programs, it's crucial to recognize that compiling extensive code takes time, and the process of identifying and rectifying errors is prolonged. Acknowledging this, it becomes imperative to accept the likelihood of encountering errors in the program.

For those inclined to undertake the creation of large programs, a prudent approach involves breaking down the code into smaller, manageable segments. Utilizing pointers to establish connections between these segments facilitates the creation of a coherent program flow. For instance, one module may be responsible for declaring variables, another for initializing them, and yet another for executing functions on the variables and displaying the results. This approach not only simplifies debugging but also offers the advantage of reusable smaller modules, potentially saving time in future projects.

When the compiler processes the source code file, it generates object code that is linked to various libraries within the programming language. Subsequently, a file is produced, which the system can execute. This linking process forms the connection between the compiler and the linker, allowing variables to be shared across different modules or source codes, enabling the execution of various functions on these shared variables.

Bitwise Logic

Employing bitwise logic in code writing allows for the setting or unsetting of bits, with some programming languages permitting the masking of specific bits. This practice is considered essential knowledge for programmers, as it enables the consolidation of multiple values into binary flags, saving these flags in the machine's memory. This approach proves efficient as it avoids the necessity for large memory chunks to store data. Furthermore, bitwise logic serves as a practical method for combining values into a single argument, transferable between methods and functions.

Beyond its fundamental uses, bitwise logic finds application in passing diverse values between web pages and other programs through cookies or query strings. Additionally, it provides a swift and straightforward means of converting variables from the denary to the binary system. Notably, bitwise logic extends its utility to text encryption purposes.

Boolean Logic

To effectively merge various values, understanding operators like AND, OR, NOT, etc., is essential. These operators simplify the creation of truth tables, a common practice among programmers. It's crucial to note that each expression must be evaluated as either true or false, and the choice of syntax depends on the programming language in use.

Closures

Closures, serving as anonymous functions or code blocks, possess the capability to be passed outside any method or function, capturing variables from the respective function or inner block. Although this might seem intricate, a practical example can clarify. Consider the code snippet below, demonstrating the use of closures in programming

```
func makeIncrementer(forIncrement amount: Int) -> () -> Int
{
  var runningTotal = 0
  func incrementer() -> Int {
  runningTotal += amount
  return runningTotal
  }
  return incrementer
}
```

let incrementByTen = makeIncrementer(forIncrement: 10)
  print("\(incrementByTen())")
  print("\(incrementByTen())")
  print("\(incrementByTen())")

The output, 10, 20, and 30, showcases the dynamic nature of the function makeIncrementer(), which utilizes 10 as the base value added by the incrementByTen() function. Additional incrementer functions, like incrementByFive, can be created to vary the increment value.

Concurrency

While concurrency shares similarities with parallel computing, it differs in that code segments are executed separately in concurrency, even if the program is running correctly. Many programming languages employ multithreading, but the recommendation is to embrace concurrency for coding. The Task Parallel Library (TPL) in C# exemplifies this approach, utilizing the CLR thread pool to run multiple processes without the need to create threads, a resource-intensive operation.

Embracing asynchronous code enhances program efficiency,

enabling simultaneous execution without hindering other code functions. In the provided example, asynchronous code and concurrency are demonstrated:

```
public async Task MethodAsync()
{
Task longRunningTask = LongRunningTaskAsync();
// ... any code here
int result = await longRunningTask;
DoSomething(result);
}

public async Task LongRunningTaskAsync() // returns an int
{
await Task.Delay(1000);
return 1;
}
```

This showcases the utilization of asynchronous code and concurrency in performing functions, enhancing responsiveness by allowing the thread to continue processing other requests while awaiting the completion of specific tasks. Concurrency proves beneficial for accessing information from different pages simultaneously, as the compiler fetches and processes pages without a predetermined order of execution due to the inherent concurrent processing nature of programming languages.

Decision-Making in Programming

It is imperative to avoid creating monolithic programs that execute only a singular action. The key lies in crafting code that exhibits flexibility, allowing for updates to accommodate diverse needs. Therefore, incorporating code capable of receiving user inputs and executing functions based on those inputs becomes crucial. Utilizing various statements, such as selection or if-else statements, enables the execution of functions or actions based on specified conditions. Additionally, lists and arrays can be employed in this process.

Disk Access

In the realm of computing, where data storage and future work on stored information are commonplace, programming languages offer functions facilitating the reading and writing of data to and from disks. However, it's essential to note that the program must be explicitly saved using the file save command for the code to persist on the computer's disk.

Immutability

Introducing immutability to certain variables in your code restricts their ability to change. Some programming languages provide specific prefixes to denote the immutability of a variable. Care should be taken to ensure no dependencies to the variable exist. While the declaration can be altered if necessary, employing immutable variables often optimizes compiler output, particularly in multi-threaded programming languages. The value of an immutable variable remains constant and can be shared between different modules and threads.

Command Line Interaction

The main function or method within a codebase plays a pivotal role, serving as the compiler's point of reference throughout the code. Every function communicates with the command line, serving as the primary means of interaction between the written code and the computer. Reading instructions from the command line is another method through which a program can communicate.

Operating System Interaction

Programming languages provide the capability to interact with the operating system to perform various functions. This interaction extends to creating and managing directories, renaming files, creating and deleting files, and executing other tasks on the operating system. Additionally, a program can run other programs using pointers, facilitating the examination of the results of functions performed by the operating system.

Lambdas

Lambdas, expressions that allow the invocation of anonymous functions during program runtime, prove invaluable, especially in languages supporting different kinds of first-class functions. With the ability to pass functions as parameters and return them as needed, lambdas originated from functional languages like C# and Lisp. Multiple languages, including PHP, Swift, Java, JavaScript, Python, and VB.NET, support lambda functions. Employing lambda functions can significantly reduce code length and enhance code readability. For instance, in building a list of odd numbers, a lambda function simplifies the process:

List list = new List() { 1, 2, 3, 4, 5, 6, 7, 8 };
List oddNumbers = list.FindAll(x => (x % 2) != 0);

The resulting oddNumbers list contains the numbers 1, 3, 5, and 7.

Iterative Structures

In coding, mastering loops and repetitions is paramount. The for loop stands out as the most prevalent iteration technique in programming, although some programmers opt for the while loop, albeit it can introduce complexity to solutions. The operation of for loops often revolves around the concept of counting iterations, with specifics varying across programming languages.

Understanding Linked Lists

Linked lists often pose a challenge due to their intricate nature. These lists require a grasp of how pointers function within them, combining the functionalities of arrays with pointers and structures. While resembling an array of structures, linked lists offer flexibility in element removal, distinguishing them from traditional data structures.

Exploring Modular Arithmetic

Modular arithmetic, involving operations on numbers within a defined modulus, provides a method to limit function outputs effectively. Employing different modular arithmetic functions allows for comprehensive wrapping of operations, rendering this technique highly advantageous. Mastery of modular arithmetic proves vital for optimal utilization within codebases.

Navigating Pointers

Pointers, ubiquitous across most programming languages, enable manipulation of variables stored in a computer's memory. Although initially daunting, understanding pointer usage empowers developers to alter variable values efficiently. Pointers enhance a language's capabilities, albeit necessitating a learning curve to harness their full potential.

Ensuring Safe Calls

Sir Tony Hoare's admonition against null references underscores the importance of exception handling in programming languages. Null references can trigger exceptions leading to program crashes, highlighting the necessity of robust exception handling mechanisms. Incorporating safety checks in programming languages mitigates null reference errors, enhancing code stability.

Harnessing Randomness and Scaling

High-level programming languages often offer libraries for generating random numbers. Understanding random number generation and scaling functions is essential for various applications, including maintaining uniformity in graphical scaling and introducing natural randomness to data structures.

Manipulating Strings

Strings represent a fundamental data type in programming, pivotal for text manipulation tasks. Defining strings involves representing sequences of characters, often achieved through character arrays. Familiarity with string manipulation functions and conventions, such as the null termination character, facilitates effective string handling in programs.

Data Structures

In programming, every language incorporates a mix of variables that can be transformed into diverse data structures. Comparable to records in databases, structures serve to describe multiple entities simultaneously. As a programmer, you have the flexibility to define and initialize data structures based on your requirements. Take, for instance, the following illustration:

```c
struct example
{
    int a;
```

```
char b;
float c;
};
"
```

In this structure, three variables are evident, each assigned a specific data type. While it's possible to create a structure with three variables without explicitly declaring them, adding declarations necessitates additional lines of code. The utility of structures extends to diverse databases contingent upon the programming language in use. Mastery of programming languages and their associated structures is crucial for effective coding.

Manipulating Text

Text manipulation stands as a pivotal concept for those delving into code, as mastering the manipulation of characters and strings is often a primary objective. A profound understanding of these concepts is imperative. Recognizing that text is stored in numerical form based on the ASCII code, it becomes essential to grasp the conversion between characters and their ASCII counterparts. This numerical representation facilitates tasks like checking letter cases or creating ciphers using bitwise exclusive OR (EOR) operations.

String manipulation functions in programming languages offer capabilities such as splitting strings using the left() and right() functions. This empowers developers to perform diverse tasks, ranging from creating anagrams to displaying specific texts on the screen. Leveraging these functions, programmers can alter letter cases and format text to enhance the visual appeal of their code or program.

Trigonometry in Programming

Comprehending trigonometry is paramount for programmers, especially when engaging in code or program development involving animation. The application of sine and cosine functions simplifies tasks such as creating circular motions, drawing patterns and circles, determining optimal object layouts on a website, and identifying angles and directions for object rotations. While computing trigonometric functions can be challenging, their incorporation significantly enhances program efficiency.

Variable Utilization

The essence of any method or function lies in producing a desired result or output. The selection of appropriate variables is crucial for achieving accurate outputs, and overlooking a variable in the code can render a program ineffective. For instance, developing a program for a mathematical function becomes futile if the output is missed due to a variable omission. Consequently, variables play a pivotal role in programming languages, with their types, declaration methods, and initialization varying across languages.

10

Testing the Program

Similar to how we assess algorithms for their efficiency, it's essential to thoroughly test any code you develop. Various testing methods and parameters can be employed for this purpose, with adherence to the Test-Driven Development (TDD) approach being crucial for code evaluation.

Principles of TDD:

1. Begin by creating a prototype of the code and writing corresponding test code. Execute and compile this test code to ensure its functionality before proceeding to write the production code.
2. Avoid writing extensive code upfront, as large codebases may result in test failures. Instead, utilize smaller code segments for testing to facilitate easier debugging and correction.
3. Upon encountering test failures, revise the test code, recompile, and then proceed to write the production code

accordingly.

When conducting code tests, it's imperative to concurrently develop the production code to guarantee its accuracy.

Maintaining Test Cleanliness:

Ensure that the tests conducted are free from errors. Test code riddled with bugs should be avoided, as it serves no purpose. Additionally, recognize that test code should evolve alongside production code changes. Designing tests meticulously and considering the process thoughtfully are essential steps. It's vital to ensure that test code mirrors the structure and integrity of the production code.

Testing Code Capabilities:

- Regardless of the code's architectural flexibility, comprehensive testing is imperative to validate its functionality and prevent production errors.
   - Unit testing verifies the code's maintainability, reusability, and flexibility. Only implement changes to the code if corresponding tests are available for assessment. Lack of test coverage necessitates manual debugging with every code alteration.

Test Quality Standards:

Clarity:
When crafting test code, prioritize readability. Ensure that the code incorporates essential attributes and remains easily comprehensible to any reader. Utilize straightforward variables and functions, clearly defining the aspects to be tested within the code.

Testing Language:
Evaluate the functionalities and utilities within specialized APIs integrated into the test code. This inclusion facilitates a better understanding of the test code and the rationale behind each code line.

Dual Standards:
Considerations must be made when developing both test and production code. Certain practices, acceptable in test code but not in production, contribute to the usability and robustness of the final production code.

Assertions:
Integrate assertions into every test code, even if it introduces some code duplication. Establish a template method as the base class, incorporating assertions across various tests. Including at least one assertion per test is crucial for effective testing.

Test Characteristics:

This segment outlines key considerations for comprehensive code testing.

Self-Validating:
Every test should yield a Boolean output, enabling straightforward validation of its effectiveness without the need to delve into logs.

Independent:
Tests should operate autonomously, devoid of dependencies on one another. Conduct tests in varying sequences to confirm the code's functionality in diverse environments.

Timeliness:
Craft tests capable of swift compilation within a few seconds. Developing test code prior to production code allows for seamless adjustments and error-free runs. Initiating test writing after commencing production code may hinder the ability to rectify errors.

Repeatability:
Endeavor to execute each test in different environments. If a test code, written for one environment, falters in others, ascertain the cause of failure.

Speed:
Optimize test speed to ensure prompt execution. Sluggish

tests may discourage frequent runs, potentially hindering effective issue identification within the code.

It is essential to recognize that the integrity of the code is contingent upon the soundness of the tests employed.

11

Sorting and Searching Algorithms

In this section, we will explore various sorting and searching algorithms, focusing on their implementation in the C programming language due to its simplicity.

Searching Algorithms:

A searching algorithm is designed to locate an element within a data structure and retrieve both the element and its position within that structure. Two main types of searching algorithms are discussed:

1. Sequential Search: This algorithm traverses the data structure sequentially, examining each element to find the target element. An example is the linear search algorithm.
2. Interval Search: An interval search algorithm operates on sorted data structures, requiring a prior sorting algorithm. It effectively searches for the target at the structure's center, with the binary search algorithm being a notable example, discussed in detail later.

Linear Search Versus Binary Search:

- Linear search scans every item in an array without requiring sorting. Its search time is directly proportional to the number of elements.
- Binary search, on the other hand, reduces search time by performing comparisons based on segments.

Key Differences:

1. Binary search requires sorting the array, whereas this is unnecessary for a linear search.
2. Linear search follows a sequential process, while binary search examines data randomly.
3. Binary search performs segment-based comparisons, while linear search uses equality comparisons.

Linear Search Example: Demonstrating a linear search on an array, consider the problem of finding the element 16 in Array1[] = {1, 4, 16, 5, 19, 10}. The linear search algorithm checks each element in the array, making it less efficient. If the target element is not present, it returns -1.

Linear Search Algorithm Steps:

1. Define the array and add numbers.
2. Identify the element to search for.
3. Begin with the leftmost element in the array.
4. Compare the target element with each array element.
5. If a match is found, return the index; otherwise, return -1.

Example Implementation in C:
#include

```c
int search(int arr[], int n, int x) {
    int i;
    for (i = 0; i < n; i++)
    if (arr[i] == x)
    return i;
    return -1;
}

int main(void) {
    int arr[] = {2, 3, 4, 10, 40};
    int x = 10;
    int n = sizeof(arr) / sizeof(arr[0]);
    int result = search(arr, n, x);
    (result == -1) ? printf("Element is not present in array")
    : printf("Element is present at index %d", result);
    return 0;
}
```

This example demonstrates the linear search algorithm in C, finding the element 10 in the array and displaying the result.

Binary Search Algorithm:

The binary search algorithm is not suitable for unsorted data. To utilize it, you must first employ a sorting algorithm to organize the data into an array. A function is then written to locate the desired element within the array. This algorithm efficiently breaks down the array into segments, conducting a linear search within each segment to find the target element.

To perform a binary search, follow these steps:

1. Define the array and list its elements, including the target element.
2. Sort the array elements and compare the target element with the middle element.
3. If the elements match, return the index or location of the target element.
4. If the target is greater than the middle element, search the right section; if lesser, search the left section.
5. Repeat steps 2-4 with the respective section of the array.
6. If the element is not found, end the search.

Implementation in C:
#include

```
int binarySearch(int arr[], int l, int r, int x) {
    if (r >= l) {
    int mid = l + (r - l) / 2;
    if (arr[mid] == x)
    return mid;
    if (arr[mid] > x)
    return binarySearch(arr, l, mid - 1, x);
    return binarySearch(arr, mid + 1, r, x);
    }
    return -1;
}

int main(void) {
```

```c
int arr[] = {2, 3, 4, 10, 40};
int n = sizeof(arr) / sizeof(arr[0]);
int x = 10;
int result = binarySearch(arr, 0, n - 1, x);
(result == -1) ? printf("Element is not present in array")
: printf("Element is present at index %d", result);
return 0;
}
```

This C program demonstrates a recursive binary search algorithm, finding the element 10 in the array and displaying the result. It emphasizes the efficiency of the binary search in ignoring elements after one comparison.

Recursive Implementation in C++:

```cpp
#include
using namespace std;

int binarySearch(int arr[], int l, int r, int x) {
    if (r >= l) {
        int mid = l + (r - l) / 2;
        if (arr[mid] == x)
            return mid;
        if (arr[mid] > x)
            return binarySearch(arr, l, mid - 1, x);
        return binarySearch(arr, mid + 1, r, x);
    }
    return -1;
}

int main(void) {
    int arr[] = {2, 3, 4, 10, 40};
    int x = 10;
```

```cpp
    int n = sizeof(arr) / sizeof(arr[0]);
    int result = binarySearch(arr, 0, n - 1, x);
    (result == -1) ? cout << "Element is not present in array"
                   : cout << "Element is present at index " << result;
    return 0;
}
```

This C++ example demonstrates the recursive binary search, displaying the output: 'Element is present at index 3'. The importance of understanding the time complexity is highlighted for efficient code compilation.

Iterative Binary Search Implementation:

```cpp
#include
using namespace std;

int binarySearch(int arr[], int l, int r, int x) {
    while (l <= r) {
        int mid = l + (r - l) / 2;
        if (arr[mid] == x)
            return mid;
        if (arr[mid] < x)
            l = mid + 1;
        else
            r = mid - 1;
    }
    return -1;
}

int main(void) {
```

```
int arr[] = {2, 3, 4, 10, 40};
int x = 10;
int n = sizeof(arr) / sizeof(arr[0]);
int result = binarySearch(arr, 0, n - 1, x);
(result == -1) ? cout << "Element is not present in array"
: cout << "Element is present at index " << result;
return 0;
}
```
The output of the code is: 'Element is present at index 3'.

Jump Search Algorithm:

The jump search algorithm, akin to binary search, seeks a specific element in a sorted array. However, it differs in its approach by searching within smaller sections of the array. This is achieved by skipping elements, leading to more efficiency than a linear search.

Example: Consider an array with elements (0, 1, 1, 2, 3, 5, 8, 13, 21, 34, 55, 89, 144, 233, 377, 610). To find the element 55, the compiler jumps ahead by four elements at a time, facilitating a quicker search.

Optimal Block Size:

Selecting an appropriate block size is crucial for the jump search algorithm's success. The block size influences the number of comparisons required. The optimal block size is $\sqrt{n}$, where 'n' is the number of elements in the array.

Implementation in C++:
```
#include
using namespace std;
```

```
int jumpSearch(int arr[], int x, int n) {
  int step = sqrt(n);
  int prev = 0;
  while (arr[min(step, n)-1] < x) {
  prev = step;
  step += sqrt(n);
  if (prev >= n)
  return -1;
  }
  while (arr[prev] < x) {
  prev++;
  if (prev == min(step, n))
  return -1;
  }
  if (arr[prev] == x)
  return prev;
  return -1;
}

int main() {
  int arr[] = {0, 1, 1, 2, 3, 5, 8, 13, 21, 34, 55, 89, 144, 233, 377, 610};
  int x = 55;
  int n = sizeof(arr) / sizeof(arr[0]);
  int index = jumpSearch(arr, x, n);
  cout « "\nNumber " « x « " is at index " « index;
  return 0;
}
```
The output of this code: 'Number 55 is at index 10'.

Key Considerations:

- Sort the array before using the algorithm.
- The optimal length to traverse is $\sqrt{n}$, resulting in a time complexity of $O(\sqrt{n})$.
- While less efficient than binary search, jump search is advantageous when minimizing memory and time is essential.

Sorting Techniques

Various sorting techniques can be employed to organize a given set of elements or an array, relying on the chosen comparison operator within the algorithm. This operator determines the arrangement of elements in the resulting data structure.

Terminology of Sorting

Before delving into the sorting algorithms available for programming, it is essential to comprehend specific terms. Two primary classifications are External and Internal Sorting. External sorting conserves memory space as it doesn't load array elements into memory, making it suitable for large datasets. Merge sort exemplifies an external sorting algorithm. Conversely, internal sorting utilizes significant memory space.

In-Place Sorting

For scenarios where only the input needs modification or the element order within the input, an in-place sorting algorithm proves beneficial. This type of algorithm solely rearranges the list of elements within the same array. Examples include selection sort and insertion sort, while merge sort and other methods do not qualify as in-place sorting algorithms.

Stability

When dealing with multiple keys within a dataset, considering the stability of the chosen algorithm is crucial. Stability ensures that duplicate keys retain their relative order during sorting, which is essential when the dataset contains keys used in subsequent operations.

Understanding Stability

In the presence of duplicate keys, a stable sorting algorithm ensures that after sorting, these keys maintain their original order. This stability condition can be defined mathematically, emphasizing the preservation of the relative positions of variables in the algorithm.

Analysis of Simple Arrays

For datasets where a single element serves as the key, stability is often a non-issue. Even with different keys, stability remains unaffected. However, when dealing with more complex datasets containing multiple keys, maintaining stability becomes imperative.

Stable and Unstable Sorting Algorithms

Stable sorting algorithms, such as Count Sort, Merge Sort, Insertion Sort, and Bubble Sort, maintain the relative order of elements. On the other hand, unstable sorting algorithms, like Heapsort and Quick Sort, can be adapted to stability by considering the relative positions of elements, ensuring performance is not compromised.

Quick Sort Algorithm

Utilizing a divide-and-conquer approach, the Quick Sort algorithm segments an array, designates a pivot element, and partitions the array based on the pivot. The choice of the pivot can vary, including options like the median, last element, any random element, or the first element. The crucial aspect lies in the partition or utility function, which orders the elements around the pivot.

Implementation:

```
#include

void swap(int* a, int* b) {
    int t = *a;
    *a = *b;
    *b = t;
}

int partition(int arr[], int low, int high) {
    int pivot = arr[high];
    int i = (low - 1);
    for (int j = low; j <= high - 1; j++) {
    if (arr[j] < pivot) {
    i++;
    swap(&arr[i], &arr[j]);
    }
    }
    swap(&arr[i + 1], &arr[high]);
    return (i + 1);
```

}

```c
void quickSort(int arr[], int low, int high) {
    if (low < high) {
    int pi = partition(arr, low, high);
    quickSort(arr, low, pi - 1);
    quickSort(arr, pi + 1, high);
    }
}

void printArray(int arr[], int size) {
    for (int i = 0; i < size; i++)
    printf("%d ", arr[i]);
    printf("\n");
}

int main() {
    int arr[] = {10, 7, 8, 9, 1, 5};
    int n = sizeof(arr) / sizeof(arr[0]);
    quickSort(arr, 0, n - 1);
    printf("Sorted array:\n");
    printArray(arr, n);
    return 0;
}
```

This Quick Sort algorithm efficiently organizes elements in an array based on the chosen pivot, demonstrating the power of the divide-and-conquer strategy in sorting.

Understanding the Partitioning Algorithm

In the quickSort function, the partition algorithm plays a crucial role in sorting an array. This algorithm efficiently places the pivot element in its correct position within the sorted array while ensuring that smaller elements are positioned to the left of the pivot and greater elements to the right.

The partition function operates by selecting the last element as the pivot. It then iterates through the array, comparing each element with the pivot. Elements smaller than the pivot are moved to the left side, while greater elements remain on the right. Finally, the pivot is placed at its correct position, separating the smaller and greater elements.

To illustrate this process, let's consider an example array: {10, 80, 30, 90, 40, 50, 70}. Initially, the pivot is set to the last element, 70. We then traverse the array, swapping elements as needed to ensure that elements smaller than the pivot are on the left and greater elements on the right. After completing the traversal, the pivot is correctly positioned, with smaller elements to its left and greater elements to its right.

The implementation of this algorithm in C++ involves defining the partition function along with the quickSort function, which recursively sorts the elements before and after the pivot.

```
#include
using namespace std;

void swap(int* a, int* b)
{
    int t = *a;
    *a = *b;
```

```
*b = t;
}

int partition(int arr[], int low, int high)
{
    int pivot = arr[high];
    int i = (low - 1);
    for (int j = low; j <= high - 1; j++)
    {
        if (arr[j] < pivot)
        {
            i++;
            swap(&arr[i], &arr[j]);
        }
    }
    swap(&arr[i + 1], &arr[high]);
    return (i + 1);
}

void quickSort(int arr[], int low, int high)
{
    if (low < high)
    {
        int pi = partition(arr, low, high);
        quickSort(arr, low, pi - 1);
        quickSort(arr, pi + 1, high);
    }
}

void printArray(int arr[], int size)
{
```

```
for (int i = 0; i < size; i++)
    cout << arr[i] << " ";
cout << endl;
}

int main()
{
    int arr[] = {10, 7, 8, 9, 1, 5};
    int n = sizeof(arr) / sizeof(arr[0]);
    quickSort(arr, 0, n - 1);
    cout << "Sorted array: \n";
    printArray(arr, n);
    return 0;
}
```

This implementation demonstrates the effective use of the partition algorithm within the quickSort function to efficiently sort an array.

Selection Sort

The selection sort algorithm divides an array into segments and sorts each segment by identifying the minimum element in the unsorted segment and relocating it to the front of the array. This process involves maintaining two segments: the sorted segment and the remaining unsorted part. In each iteration, the algorithm moves the minimum element from the unsorted segment to the sorted one.

Illustrating this with an example: consider the array **array1[]** = **{10, 65, 40, 12, 22}**. The algorithm locates the minimum element, in this case, 10, and places it at the beginning. Subsequently, it continues to identify and move the minimum elements, resulting in a sorted array: **{10, 12, 22, 40, 65}**.

Implementation

```c
#include

int main() {
    int i, j, count, temp, number[25];
    printf("Number of elements: ");
    scanf("%d", &count);
    printf("Enter %d elements: ", count);

// Loop to get the elements stored in the array
    for(i = 0; i < count; i++)
    scanf("%d", &number[i]);

// Logic of selection sort algorithm
    for(i = 0; i < count; i++) {
    for(j = i + 1; j < count; j++) {
    if(number[i] > number[j]) {
    temp = number[i];
    number[i] = number[j];
    number[j] = temp;
    }
    }
    }

    printf("Sorted elements: ");
    for(i = 0; i < count; i++)
    printf(" %d", number[i]);

    return 0;
}
```

Bubble Sort

The bubble sort algorithm is a straightforward sorting technique. It compares adjacent elements, sorting them in ascending order. If the elements are already in the correct position, no further action is taken. The process involves defining the array, calculating its length, and then iterating through the array elements, comparing and swapping adjacent elements as needed.

For example, given the array {64, 34, 25, 12, 22, 11, 90}, the bubble sort algorithm makes multiple passes, swapping adjacent elements until the entire array is sorted.

Implementation

```
#include
using namespace std;

void swap(int *xp, int *yp) {
    int temp = *xp;
    *xp = *yp;
    *yp = temp;
}

void bubbleSort(int arr[], int n) {
    int i, j;
    for (i = 0; i < n - 1; i++)
    for (j = 0; j < n - i - 1; j++)
    if (arr[j] > arr[j + 1])
    swap(&arr[j], &arr[j + 1]);
}

void printArray(int arr[], int size) {
    for (int i = 0; i < size; i++)
```

```
        cout « arr[i] « " ";
        cout « endl;
    }

int main() {
    int arr[] = {64, 34, 25, 12, 22, 11, 90};
    int n = sizeof(arr) / sizeof(arr[0]);
    bubbleSort(arr, n);
    cout « "Sorted array: \n";
    printArray(arr, n);
    return 0;
}
```

Insertion Sort

The insertion sort algorithm, inspired by sorting playing cards, is simple and effective. It involves creating an array, then using a loop to iterate through the elements, choosing each element and inserting it into the sorted sequence. The array is modified based on its size, and the algorithm concludes once all elements are considered.

For instance, given **Array1[] = {12, 11, 13, 5, 6}**, the algorithm progressively inserts each element into its correct position, resulting in the sorted array **{5, 6, 11, 12, 13}**.

Implementation

```
#include

void insertionSort(int arr[], int n) {
    int i, key, j;
    for (i = 1; i < n; i++) {
    key = arr[i];
    j = i - 1;
    while (j >= 0 && arr[j] > key) {
```

```
    arr[j + 1] = arr[j];
    j = j - 1;
    }
    arr[j + 1] = key;
    }
}

void printArray(int arr[], int n) {
    int i;
    for (i = 0; i < n; i++)
    printf("%d ", arr[i]);
    printf("\n");
}

int main() {
    int arr[] = {12, 11, 13, 5, 6};
    int n = sizeof(arr) / sizeof(arr[0]);
    insertionSort(arr, n);
    printArray(arr, n);
    return 0;
}
```

Merge Sort

Similar to the quicksort algorithm, the mergesort algorithm is also a divide-and-conquer approach. In this sorting technique, the input array undergoes division into two halves. The sorting algorithm is invoked to sort the elements within each half, followed by merging the arrays into a single sorted array. The merging process is accomplished using the merge function, requiring the following parameters:

1. The input array with its elements.
2. The first sorted half.
3. The second sorted half.

To apply the mergesort algorithm:

1. Define the array and populate it with elements.
2. Divide the array into halves, sorting each half's elements.
3. Utilize the merge function to combine the sorted arrays.
4. Conclude the algorithm.

Implementation

```
// In this code, two subarrays of array arr[] will be merged. The first
// subarray is arr[l..m], and the second is arr[m+1..r]
void merge(int arr[], int l, int m, int r) {
int i, j, k;
int n1 = m - l + 1;
int n2 = r - m;
/* create temp arrays */
int L[n1], R[n2];
/* Copy data to temp arrays L[] and R[] */
for (i = 0; i < n1; i++)
L[i] = arr[l + i];
for (j = 0; j < n2; j++)
R[j] = arr[m + 1 + j];
/* Merge the temp arrays back into arr[l..r]*/
i = 0; // Initial index of the first subarray
j = 0; // Initial index of the second subarray
k = l; // Initial index of the merged subarray
```

```
while (i < n1 && j < n2) {
if (L[i] <= R[j]) {
arr[k] = L[i];
i++;
} else {
arr[k] = R[j];
j++;
}
k++;
}
/* Copy the remaining elements of L[], if there
are any */
while (i < n1) {
arr[k] = L[i];
i++;
k++;
}
/* Copy the remaining elements of R[], if there
are any */
while (j < n2) {
arr[k] = R[j];
j++;
k++;
}
}
/* l is for the left index and r is the right index of the
sub-array of arr to be sorted */
void mergeSort(int arr[], int l, int r) {
if (l < r) {
// Avoid overflow for large l and h
int m = l + (r - l) / 2;
```

```c
// Sort first and second halves
mergeSort(arr, l, m);
mergeSort(arr, m + 1, r);
merge(arr, l, m, r);
    }
}

/* UTILITY FUNCTIONS */
/* Function to print an array */
void printArray(int A[], int size) {
    int i;
    for (i = 0; i < size; i++)
        printf("%d ", A[i]);
    printf("\n");
}

/* Driver program to test above functions */
int main() {
    int arr[] = {12, 11, 13, 5, 6, 7};
    int arr_size = sizeof(arr) / sizeof(arr[0]);
    printf("Given array is \n");
    printArray(arr, arr_size);
    mergeSort(arr, 0, arr_size - 1);
    printf("\nSorted array is \n");
    printArray(arr, arr_size);
    return 0;
}
```

This implementation effectively demonstrates the merge sort algorithm's step-by-step process of dividing, sorting, and merging, resulting in a sorted array.

12

Loop Control and Decision Making

As previously mentioned, the majority of algorithms incorporate loops and conditional statements. Thus, it's crucial to comprehend how to implement these algorithms in any programming language. Programming languages execute code sequentially, meaning the compiler processes each statement in order. However, you can influence this sequence using loops and conditionals, enabling you to execute complex operations on data.

Decision-making is fundamental in programming, requiring programmers to adeptly utilize conditional statements to execute specific functions. These statements entail evaluating one or more conditions and executing corresponding statements based on their values. Additionally, programmers can include statements to execute if the condition is false. Most programming languages feature several decision-making statements:

- ?: Operator:

This conditional operator, akin to an if…else statement, evaluates expressions in the format: State1? State2 : State3; where State1, State2, and State3 are expressions. The outcome depends on the evaluation of State1: if true, State2's value becomes the result; if false, State3's value prevails.

- If Statement:

The ubiquitous decision-making statement in programming, it consists of a Boolean expression and one or more statements within its body.

- If Else Statement:

Optionally succeeding an if statement, an else statement executes when the Boolean expression evaluates as false.

- Nested If:

Employed for testing multiple conditions, a nested if statement allows the inclusion of multiple if statements and one else statement.

- Switch Statement:

Used to compare a variable against a list of predetermined values for equality.

Loop Statements

To repetitively execute statements within a section of code, loops are employed. The three common types of loops found in most programming languages are:

1. For Loop
2. While Loop
3. Do While Loop

For Loop:

Executing a statement multiple times based on specified parameters, the for loop employs a loop variable to control its iterations. The syntax of the for loop is as follows:
for (initialization; condition; update)
{
Body;
}
In the for loop, the loop variable is initialized in the function's parameters, and its value is modified within the loop's body. The condition, resulting in a Boolean output (true or false), determines the number of iterations. If the condition evaluates to false, the loop breaks, and statements following the loop are executed. If the condition persists, the loop continues indefinitely.

Consider the following example, where a for loop is utilized to print numbers 0 – 10:

```
for (int i = 0; i <= 10; i++)
{
Console.Write(i + " ");
}
```

The for loop can be employed for intricate functions, such as calculating the power (m) of a number (n).

While Loop:

The while loop repeats one or more statements in its body based on a specified condition. The condition is evaluated before executing the loop body. The syntax is as follows:

```
while (condition)
{
Body;
}
```

In the example below, a while loop is used to print numbers 0 – 9:

```
int count = 0;
while (count <= 9)
{
Console.WriteLine("Number : " + count);
count++;
}
```

The while loop can also calculate the sum of numbers or perform other mathematical calculations.

Do While Loop:

Similar to the while loop, the do…while loop executes its body before testing the condition. This guarantees the loop runs at least once, even if the initial condition is false. The syntax is as follows:

```
do
{
Body;
} while (condition);
```

In the following example, a do while loop is used to calculate the factorial of a number:

```
int n = int.Parse(Console.ReadLine());
    BigInteger factorial = 1;
    do
    {
    factorial *= n;
    n—;
    } while (n > 0);
    Console.WriteLine("n! = " + factorial);
```

This program calculates the factorial of a user-specified number.

Loop Control Statements

Loop control statements are employed to alter the regular sequence of execution. Upon completing its designated task, the execution exits its scope, leading to the automatic destruction of all objects created within that scope.

The following control statements are commonly supported in various programming languages:

Break Statement:

Utilized to exit a loop prematurely, the break statement proves useful in scenarios where incorrect code may cause an infinite loop. Placed within the loop, it terminates the ongoing iteration, and any code following the break statement is disregarded. An illustration is provided in the code snippet below, demonstrating the calculation of the factorial of a number:

```
int n = int.Parse(Console.ReadLine());
decimal factorial = 1;
while (true)
{
if (n <= 1)
{
break;
}
factorial *= n;
n—;
}
Console.WriteLine("n! = " + factorial);
```

In this example, the break statement halts the loop when the value of **n** becomes less than or equal to 1.

Foreach Loop:

An extension of the for loop, the foreach loop is widely used in programming languages like C, C++, C#, PHP, and VB. It simplifies iterating over all elements in an array or list without the need for indexing. The syntax is as follows:

foreach (type variable in the collection)
  {
  Body;
  }

The foreach loop is favored by many programmers for its efficiency. The subsequent example demonstrates its usage:

int[] numbers = { 2, 3, 5, 7, 11, 13, 17, 19 };
foreach (int i in numbers)
{
Console.Write(" " + i);
}
Console.WriteLine();
string[] towns = { "London", "Paris", "Milan", "New York" };
foreach (string town in towns)
{
Console.Write(" " + town);
}

Nested Loops:

A nested loop contains multiple loops within the main loop. The syntax is as follows:

for (initialization, verification, update)

```
{
for (initialization, verification, update)
{
Body;
}
}
```

Before implementing nested loops, it is crucial to outline the algorithm and determine the organizational structure of the loops. For instance, to print numbers in a specific format, two loops are needed—one for lines and another for elements within each line.

Continue Statement:

The continue statement allows the loop to skip the remaining loop body and reevaluate the condition before proceeding with the next iteration. The following example illustrates its functionality:

```
int n = int.Parse(Console.ReadLine());
  int sum = 0;
  for (int i = 1; i <= n; i += 2)
  {
  if (i % 8 == 0)
  {
  continue;
  }
  sum += i;
  }
  Console.WriteLine("sum = " + sum);
```

In this program, the continue statement excludes numbers divisible by 8 from contributing to the sum, thus altering the loop's behavior.

13

Introduction to Data Structures

Data Structure Usage and Struct Statement

In various programming languages, the utilization of data structures like lists and arrays was briefly explored in the eighth chapter. This chapter delves into different methods for defining and employing data structures, demonstrating how they can be employed to manage multiple variables or combine diverse elements, be they input or output variables, throughout an entire program. Unlike a simple variable, a structure allows the amalgamation of different variables and data types, providing a means to define or represent records. To illustrate, envision organizing a library bookshelf; a data structure can efficiently track distinct attributes for each book. For this instance, the attributes include:

1. Book ID
2. Book title
3. Genre

4. Author

The Struct Statement precedes the definition of any data structure, crucial for creating it in the program. It's essential to note that the struct statement is exclusive to C and C++ languages, while other languages may employ different statements. The structure is defined using the following syntax:

struct [structure tag] {
member definition;
member definition;
...
member definition;
} [one or more structure variables];

The structure tag is optional, and each member is defined using the variable definition method. Continuing with the bookshelf example, the book structure is defined with the following code:

struct Books {
　int book_id;
　char book_title[50];
　char genre[50];
　char author[100];
} book;

Accessing structure members is achieved through the member access operator, denoted by a full stop. It acts as a separator between data structure members and variable names. The example continues with code lines demonstrating the usage of structures:

```cpp
#include
  #include
  using namespace std;

struct Books {
  int book_id;
  char book_title[60];
  char genre[60];
  char author[40];
};

int main() {
  struct Books Book1;
  struct Books Book2;

// Adding details to the first variable
  Book1.book_id = 1001;
  strcpy(Book1.book_title, "Eragon");
  strcpy(Book1.genre, " Fantasy");
  strcpy(Book1.author, "Christopher Paolini");

// Adding data to the second variable
  Book2.book_id = 1002;
  strcpy(Book2.book_title, "Eldest");
  strcpy(Book2.genre, "Fantasy");
  strcpy(Book2.author, "Christopher Paolini");

// Printing details of the first and second variables
  cout « "Book 1 id: " « Book1.book_id « endl;
  cout « "Book 1 title: " « Book1.book_title « endl;
  cout « "Book 1 genre: " « Book1.genre « endl;
```

```
cout << "Book 1 author: " << Book1.author << endl;
cout << "Book 2 id: " << Book2.book_id << endl;
cout << "Book 2 title: " << Book2.book_title << endl;
cout << "Book 2 genre: " << Book2.genre << endl;
cout << "Book 2 author: " << Book2.author << endl;

return 0;
}
```

The output displays details for both Book1 and Book2 in the specified data structure format.

Utilizing Structures as Function Arguments

A data structure can function as an argument in a function, much like passing variables or pointers as parameters. To implement this, access the variables as demonstrated in the preceding example.

```
#include
#include
using namespace std;

struct Books {
  int book_id;
  char book_title[60];
  char genre[60];
  char author[40];
};

int main() {
  struct Books Book1; // Declaration of the first variable, Book1, in the data structure.
```

```
    struct Books Book2; // Declaration of the second variable,
Book2, in the data structure.

    // Adding details to the first variable
    Book1.book_id = 1001;
    strcpy(Book1.book_title, "Eragon");
    strcpy(Book1.genre, " Fantasy");
    strcpy(Book1.author, "Christopher Paolini");

    // Adding data to the second variable
    Book2.book_id = 1002;
    strcpy(Book2.book_title, "Eldest");
    strcpy(Book2.genre, "Fantasy");
    strcpy(Book2.author, "Christopher Paolini");

    // Updating details of the second variable
    Book2.book_id = 130000;
    strcpy(Book2.book_title, "Harry Potter and the Chamber of Secrets");
    strcpy(Book2.genre, "Fiction");
    strcpy(Book2.author, "JK Rowling");

    // Printing details of the first and second variables in the structure
    printBook(Book1);
    printBook(Book2);

    return 0;
}

void printBook(struct Books book) {
```

cout « "Book id: " « book.book_id « endl;
cout « "Book title: " « book.book_title « endl;
cout « "Book genre: " « book.genre « endl;
cout « "Book author: " « book.author « endl;
}

When you compile the code, the output will be as follows:

Book 1 id: 120000
Book 1 title: Harry Potter and the Philosopher's Stone
Book 1 genre: Fiction
Book 1 author: JK Rowling
Book 2 id: 130000
Book 2 title: Harry Potter and the Chamber of Secrets
Book 2 genre: Fiction
Book 2 author: JK Rowling

Using Pointers with Structures

Structures can also be referenced using pointers, much like regular variables. A pointer variable is defined using the following statement:

struct Books *struct_pointer;

This pointer variable can store the address of the variables within the structure, and you can access structure members using the -> operator. The code example below demonstrates using pointers with structures:

```
#include
  #include
  using namespace std;
```

```c
struct Books {
  int book_id;
  char book_title[50];
  char genre[50];
  char author[100];
};

void printBook(struct Books *book);

int main() {
  struct Books Book1; // Declaration of the variable Book1 in the Book structure
  struct Books Book2; // Declaration of the variable Book2 in the Book structure

  // Adding details to the first variable
  Book1.book_id = 1001;
  strcpy(Book1.book_title, "Eragon");
  strcpy(Book1.genre, "Fantasy");
  strcpy(Book1.author, "Christopher Paolini");

  // Adding details to the second variable
  Book2.book_id = 1002;
  strcpy(Book2.book_title, "Eldest");
  strcpy(Book2.genrc, "Fantasy");
  strcpy(Book2.author, "Christopher Paolini");

  // Printing details of the first and second variables in the structure using a pointer
  printBook(&Book1);
  printBook(&Book2);
```

```
return 0;
}
```

```
void printBook(struct Books *book) {
    cout << "Book id: " << book->book_id << endl;
    cout << "Book title: " << book->book_title << endl;
    cout << "Book genre: " << book->genre << endl;
    cout << "Book author: " << book->author << endl;
}
```

The output of the above code will be:

```
Book id: 1001
Book title: Eragon
Book genre: Fantasy
Book author: Christopher Paolini
Book id: 1002
Book title: Eldest
Book genre: Fantasy
Book author: Christopher Paolini
```

Type Definition Keyword

When faced with difficulty defining a data structure using conventional methods, employ an alias structure using the typedef keyword. Take the following illustration into consideration:

```
typedef struct {
int book_id;
char book_title[50];
char genre[50];
char author[100];
```

} Books;

This approach simplifies the structure definition, allowing you to declare variables within the structure without the need for the struct keyword:

Books Book1, Book2;

It's important to note that the typedef keyword is not exclusive to defining data structures; it can also be utilized for regular variables. For instance:

```
typedef long int *pint32;
   pint32 x, y, z;
```

In the above code, the compiler associates with the variables x, y, and z.

14

Comments and Formatting

In this section, we'll delve into key aspects of writing comments and formatting code. While the algorithm forms the backbone of code, it's essential to articulate each significant step within the algorithm during the coding process. This elucidates the code for readers, facilitating comprehension. Incorporate comments judiciously, emphasizing the importance of regular code review for readability and understanding. Adhering to code formatting and indentation is paramount.

Comments

Effectively crafting comments requires understanding. The common dilemma pertains to the quantity of comments; excessive comments may lead to oversight during code modification. Educating programmers on comment upkeep is challenging. Updates to the code must parallel comment revisions to prevent discrepancies. Consider comments as documentation, essential for clarifying code functionality.

Features of Good Comments

Clarification and Intention:

1. Comments should elucidate the coder's intent, not necessarily every line of code. Express actions and reasons behind specific choices, aiding comprehension.

```
// Code to check if the input variables are valid
function is_valid($first_name, $last_name, $age) {
// Code logic for validation
return true;
}
```

Informative and Legal:

1. Comments may be mandated by laws or serve documentation purposes. Specify license terms and link to external resources. Convey method information and return values when relevant.

Features of Bad Comments

Adding Unnecessary Comments:

- Superfluous comments clutter the code, impeding readability. Reserve comments for essential explanations, avoiding information overload.

Code Explanation:

- Difficulty in explaining code may stem from its complexity. Rather than relying on comments, refactor the code with meaningful names for functions, variables, and objects.

Redundant:

- Descriptive naming eliminates the need for redundant comments. Clearly named methods or fields render additional explanations unnecessary.

Position Markers:

- Refrain from using markers like ///// in code. Modern tools enable efficient code navigation, making such markers obsolete.

Journal:

- Documenting code changes is crucial. Utilize journaling mechanisms within programming languages, eliminating the need for comments to track modifications.

Mandated, Noise, and Misleading:

- Inconsequential comments lack value. Avoid vague comments that merely state routine operations without explaining their purpose.

Ugly Code:

- Comments should not serve as a bandage for convoluted or unreadable code. Instead, focus on refactoring and enhancing code clarity.

Adhering to these principles ensures that comments enhance code readability and provide valuable insights without introducing unnecessary complexity.

Formatting and Code Style

When writing code, it's crucial to adhere to a consistent formatting style. This becomes especially important when collaborating with a team; make sure everyone follows the agreed-upon style. Avoid spending unnecessary time on formatting by choosing a style upfront and sticking to it. Numerous examples in this book and various formats on the internet can guide you. Resist changing formatting styles midway through coding, and understand your team members' preferences to embrace evolving coding standards. Alongside formatting, focus on writing clear and well-organized code.

Functions

Functions within code often rely on each other, inheriting functionalities or values from other modules. Organize these functions hierarchically, placing child functions within parent functions. This practice streamlines code readability, eliminating the need to extensively navigate through the code to locate related functions.

Indentation

Consistent indentation is a fundamental aspect of coding. Adhere to established indentation standards even when making exceptions. Following consistent indentation rules aids in quickly identifying variables and other essential elements of the code. Utilize modern tools and Integrated Development Environments (IDEs) to seamlessly maintain uniform indentation throughout the codebase.

Code Affinity

Efficiently organize code with a shared purpose, including variables, functions, and objects, within dedicated sections. Avoid scattering code throughout a file, necessitating excessive scrolling to locate specific functionality. Concentrate related code in specific sections to enhance code readability and accessibility.

15

Debugging

Efficient Code Debugging

Avoid excessive time spent on debugging; anticipate errors and handle them strategically. Follow the steps outlined below to streamline the debugging process, ensuring effective code assessment and necessary modifications for error-free compilation.

1. Understand the Algorithm and Design

Fully comprehend the algorithm before coding to prevent unintended actions. If using someone else's code as a reference, review the algorithm, design, and comments. Understanding the algorithm is essential for developing effective test cases, especially when utilizing data structures.

2. Check Code Correctness

Utilize different methods to verify code correctness and ensure error-free compilation.

3. Peer Reviews

Engage a knowledgeable peer to review your code thoroughly. Provide necessary information, including comments, and explain the algorithm. Encourage open communication to address disagreements or misunderstandings. The peer's objective is error detection, facilitating accurate corrections.

4. Code Tracing

Detect errors by tracing the execution of various functions and modules, particularly when calls are made from different program sections. Assume the accuracy of other functions and procedures during code tracing, dealing with varying layers of inheritance and abstraction.

5. Proof of Correctness

Examine the algorithm and validate its correctness using different methods. Evaluate loop statements based on preconditions, terminating conditions, invariants, and postconditions. Ask specific questions to assess the accuracy of the code and gain a deeper understanding of the algorithm.

Anticipate Errors

Recognize the possibility of errors in coding, such as using incorrect pointers or variables, forgetting function calls, or making mistakes during code tracing. Be prepared for these errors and employ error-handling techniques discussed earlier in the book. Embrace errors as opportunities for improvement rather than viewing them as unfortunate incidents.

16

Conclusions

Thank you for acquiring this book. If you are a beginner in programming, it's crucial to grasp the mechanics of algorithms and apply them in your coding endeavors. This guide encompasses all the details you need for structuring your programs. It acquaints you with the fundamentals of algorithms and demonstrates their utilization in crafting efficient code. Sorting and searching algorithms are also introduced.

Leverage the insights and examples provided in this book to enhance your comprehension of algorithms. Through practice, cultivate the skill of coding to achieve superior performance compared to your previous coding endeavors.

I trust that you have found the information you sought within these pages.

www.ingramcontent.com/pod-product-compliance
Lightning Source LLC
LaVergne TN
LVHW011952070526
838202LV00054B/4905